No Backbone!
The World of Invertebrates

Beautiful Butterflies

by Meish Goldish

Consultant: Brian V. Brown
Curator, Entomology Section
Natural History Museum of Los Angeles County

BEARPORT
PUBLISHING

NEW YORK, NEW YORK

Credits

Cover, © Tan Kian Khoon/Shutterstock; 4T, © Symon Lobsang/Workbook Stock/Jupiterimages; 4C, © Ross Hoddinott/
Nature Picture Library; 4B, © Nick Garbutt/Nature Picture Library; 5, © age fotostock/SuperStock; 6, © De Meester/
ARCO/Nature Picture Library; 7, © Darrell Gulin/Jupiterimages; 8, © Chris Evans, River to River CWMA, Bugwood.org; 9,
© Larry F. Jernigan/Jupiterimages; 10, © John Cancalosi/Nature Picture Library; 11, © M. & C. Photography/Peter Arnold
Inc.; 12, © Wegner/ARCO/Nature Picture Library; 13, © A. Krieger/Peter Arnold; 14, © Brian Kenney/Oxford Scientific
Films/Photolibrary; 15, © Natural Selection/Creatas Images/Jupiterimages; 16, © Michael Durham/Nature Picture
Library; 17, © Michael Durham/Nature Picture Library; 19, © Hans Christoph Kappel/Nature Picture Library; 20–21, ©
Creatas/SuperStock; 22TL, © Scott Camazine/Photo Researchers, Inc.; 22TR, © Biophoto Associates/Photo Researchers,
Inc; 22BL, © Todd Taulman/Shutterstock; 22BR, © David Cappaert, Michigan State University, Bugwood.org; 23TL, ©
Jim Wehtje/Photodisc Green/Getty Images; 23TR, © Natural Selection/Creatas Images/Jupiterimages; 23BL, © Michael
Durham/Nature Picture Library; 23BR, © Darrell Gulin/Jupiterimages.

Publisher: Kenn Goin
Editorial Director: Adam Siegel
Creative Director: Spencer Brinker
Design: Dawn Beard Creative
Photo Researcher: Beaura Kathy Ringrose

Library of Congress Cataloging-in-Publication Data

Goldish, Meish.
  Beautiful butterflies / by Meish Goldish.
    p. cm. — (No backbone! The world of invertebrates series)
  Includes bibliographical references and index.
  ISBN-13: 978-1-59716-587-7 (library binding)
  ISBN-10: 1-59716-587-5 (library binding)
  1. Butterflies—Juvenile literature. I. Title.

  QL544.2.G65 2008
  595.78'9—dc22

                      2007037578

For more information, write to Bearport Publishing Company, Inc., 101 Fifth Avenue, Suite 6R,
New York, New York 10003. Printed in the United States of America.

10 9 8 7 6 5 4 3 2 1

Contents

Pretty Colors

Butterflies are flying **insects** with large, pretty wings.

They can be different sizes and colors.

Some butterflies are yellow, like butter.

That may be how the insects got their name.

There are more than 18,000 kinds of butterflies.

A Butterfly's Body

Like all insects, butterflies have six legs and two antennas.

They use their antennas for smelling and their legs for walking.

They also do something unusual with their two front feet.

They use them to taste their food!

Butterflies and all other insects have a hard covering called an exoskeleton. The exoskeleton protects the soft inner parts of an insect's body.

antennas

legs

7

Feeding from Flowers

A butterfly has a long, thin beak.

Usually, it is curled up.

The butterfly uncurls its beak when it eats.

It uses its beak like a straw to suck up a sweet liquid called nectar from flowers.

Nectar is the only food that most butterflies eat.

curled beak

Butterflies also use their long beaks to sip drops of water from the wet ground.

beak

Scary Colors

Many insects and birds like to eat butterflies.

However, many butterflies have colors that help them stay safe.

Some poisonous butterflies are bright orange or yellow with black.

Enemies that try to eat one of them never try again.

They remember the butterfly's bad taste and bright colors, and they stay away.

Some butterflies have spots on their wings that look like big eyes. These scary-looking markings may help keep enemies away, too.

poisonous
butterfly

Eggs on Leaves

A female butterfly lays her eggs on a plant leaf.

When the babies hatch, they will eat the leaves of the plant.

So the female must find the right kind of plant.

Often, she tastes the leaves with her feet to make sure they will be good to eat.

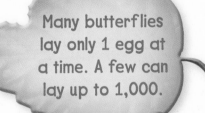

Many butterflies lay only 1 egg at a time. A few can lay up to 1,000.

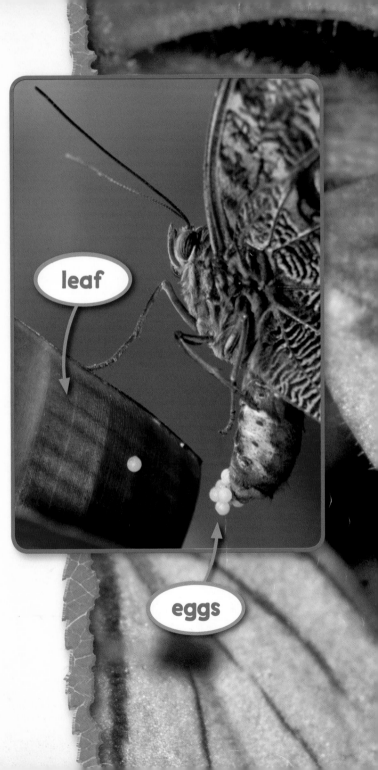

leaf

eggs

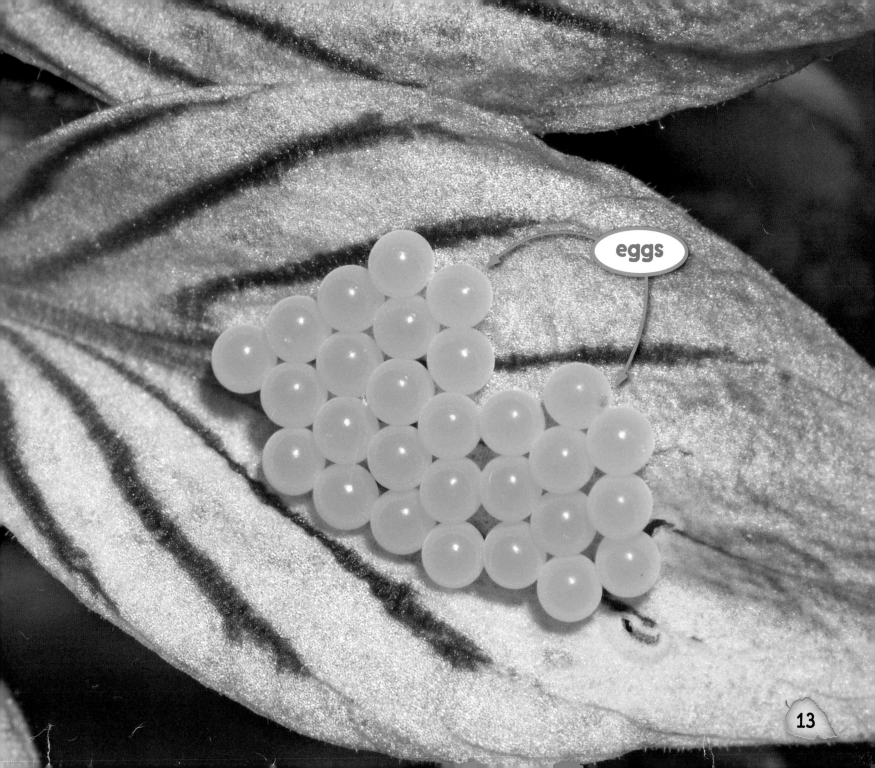

eggs

Hungry Crawlers

When a butterfly egg hatches, a **caterpillar** crawls out.

The hungry worm-like creature first eats its own shell.

Then it eats leaves on the plant where it hatched.

It eats and grows until its exoskeleton splits open.

The caterpillar is now protected by a new exoskeleton that has been growing underneath.

eggshell

caterpillar

Shedding and growing an exoskeleton is called molting. Caterpillars molt about four times as they grow bigger.

A Big Change

After its last molt, a caterpillar attaches itself to a leaf or branch.

It uses little hooks on its body to hang upside down.

A hard shell called a **chrysalis** now covers its body.

Inside the shell, the young insect changes its shape completely.

When the shell splits open, an adult butterfly comes out!

chrysalis

It takes from a few days to a year for a caterpillar to change into an adult butterfly. The amount of time depends on the kind of butterfly that is forming in the chrysalis.

16

adult Monarch
butterfly

Amazing Travelers

The most famous kind of butterfly in North America is the Monarch.

In the fall, millions of Monarchs leave places that will get cold in the winter.

They fly to warm winter homes far away.

In the spring, they lay their eggs as they make the long trip back.

The adults die along the way, but the babies live on.

CANADA

UNITED STATES

California

MEXICO

Florida

Atlantic Ocean

Pacific Ocean

Where Monarchs fly in the fall

N
W E
S

Many Monarchs travel more than 2,000 miles (3,219 km). They fly from Canada and the northern United States to warm places in Florida, California, and Mexico.

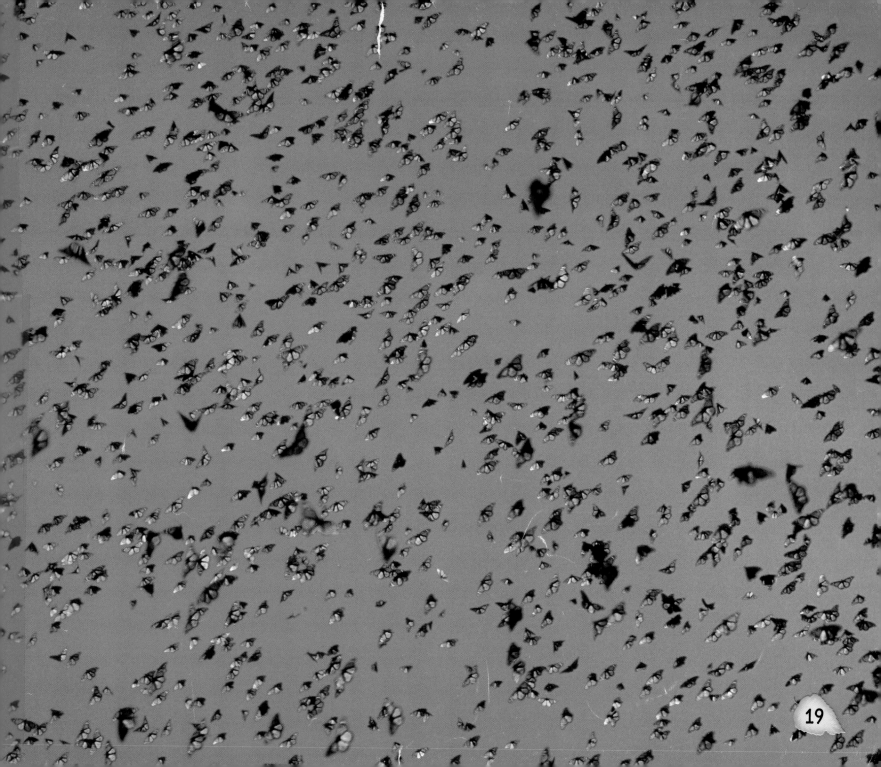

A World of Color

Butterflies are important insects.

As they fly among plants, they spread a powder from flowers called pollen.

Pollen helps new plants to grow.

These colorful insects add beauty to the world in more ways than one!

Butterflies live all over the world—from hot deserts to cold mountains. They live wherever they can find plants for food.

A World of Invertebrates

An animal that has a skeleton with a **backbone** inside its body is a *vertebrate* (VUR-tuh-brit). Mammals, birds, fish, reptiles, and amphibians are all vertebrates.

An animal that does not have a skeleton with a backbone inside its body is an *invertebrate* (in-VUR-tuh-brit). More than 95 percent of all kinds of animals on Earth are invertebrates.

Some invertebrates, such as insects and spiders, have hard skeletons—called exoskeletons—on the outside of their bodies. Other invertebrates, such as worms and jellyfish, have soft, squishy bodies with no exoskeletons to protect them.

Here are four insects that are closely related to butterflies. Like all insects, they are invertebrates.

Gypsy Moth

Tiger Moth

Luna Moth

Skipper

Glossary

backbone
(BAK-*bohn*)
a group of connected bones that run along the backs of some animals, such as dogs, cats, and fish; also called a spine

caterpillar
(KAT-ur-*pil*-ur)
a worm-like creature that changes into a butterfly

chrysalis
(KRISS-uh-liss)
a hard shell that protects a caterpillar as it changes into a butterfly

insects (IN-sekts)
small animals that have six legs, three main body parts, two antennas, and a hard covering called an exoskeleton

Index

Read More

Brimner, Larry Dane. *Butterflies and Moths.* New York: Children's Press (1999).

Kelly, Irene. *It's a Butterfly's Life.* New York: Holiday House (2007).

Turnbull, Stephanie. *Caterpillars and Butterflies.* London: Usborne (2007).

Learn More Online

To learn more about butterflies, visit

www.bearportpublishing.com/NoBackbone-Insects

About the Author

Meish Goldish has written more than 100 books for children. He lives in Brooklyn, New York, where many beautiful butterflies can be seen.